LEARNING ALPHABET WITH FRUITS AND VEGETABLES

THOMAS ABRAHAM

SUNIPRINT
A Division of Abraham Thomas Foundation

LEARNING ALPHABET WITH FRUITS AND VEGETABLES

Copyright © SUNIPRINT
2023

All rights reserved. This publication may not be reproduced, distributed or transmitted in any from or by any means including photocopying, recording, or other electronic or mechanical methods without the prior written permission of the publisher.

Layout: Sunil Thomas

ISBN: 979-8-9866300-4-5

SUNIPRINT
A Division of Abraham Thomas Foundation
11 Cambridge Road, Broomall,
PA-19008, USA
E-mail: suniprintbooks@gmail.com

A a

APPLE

apple

APRICOT

apricot

ARTICHOKE

artichoke

ARUGULA

arugula

ASPARAGUS

asparagus

AVOCADO

avocado

B b

BABACO

babaco

BACURI

bacuri

BALSAM APPLE

balsam apple

BAMBOO SHOOT

bamboo shoot

BANANA

banana

BEANS

beans

BEETROOT

beetroot

BELL PEPPER

bell pepper

BITTER GOURD

bitter gourd

BLACKBERRY

blackberry

BLUEBERRY

blueberry

BOK CHOY

bok choy

BOSTON LETTUCE

Boston lettuce

BOYSENBERRY

boysenberry

BREADFRUIT

breadfruit

BROCCOLI RABE

broccoli rabe

BROCCOLI

broccoli

BRUSSELS SPROUT

Brussels sprout

C c

CABBAGE

cabbage

CALABASH

calabash

CAMU CAMU BERRY

camu camu berry

CANARY MELON

canary melon

CANTALOUPE

cantaloupe

CARROT

carrot

CAULIFLOWER

cauliflower

CELERY

celery

CHERRY

cherry

CLEMENTINE

clementine

COCOA

cocoa

COCONUT

coconut

COLLARD GREEN

collard green

CORN

corn

CRANBERRY

cranberry

CRESS

cress

CUCUMBER

cucumber

CUPCAKE FRUIT

cupcake fruit

D d

DAIKON RADISH

daikon radish

DAMSON

damson

DATES

dates

DELICATA SQUASH

delicata squash

DEWBERRY

dewberry

DILL

dill

DRAGON FRUIT

dragon fruit

DURIAN

durian

E e

EGGPLANT

eggplant

ELDERBERRY

elderberry

ENDIVE

endive

ESCAROLE LETTUCE

escarole lettuce

F f

FAIRCHILD TANGERINE

Fairchild tangerine

FEIJOA

feijoa

FIG

fig

FINGER LIME

finger lime

FRENCH BEANS

French beans

G g

GARDEN PEA

garden pea

GARDEN ROCKET

garden rocket

GRAPEFRUIT

grapefruit

GRAPES

grapes

GREEN BELL PEPPER

green bell pepper

GUAVA

guava

H h

HACKBERRY

hackberry

HAWTHORN

hawthorn

HEIRLOOM TOMATO

heirloom tomato

HONEYCRISP APPLE

honeycrisp apple

HORSERADISH
horseradish

I i

ICEBERG LETTUCE

iceberg lettuce

INDIAN JUJUBE

Indian jujube

INDIAN PRUNE

Indian prune

INDIAN SHERBET BERRY

Indian sherbet berry

ITALIAN RED ONION

Italian red onion

J j

JACKFRUIT

jackfruit

JALAPEÑO CHILI PEPPER

jalapeño chili pepper

JAPANESE MUSTARD SPINACH

Japanese mustard spinach

JICAMA

jicama

K k

KABOCHA SQUASH

kabocha squash

KALE

kale

KARONDA

karonda

KEY LIME

key lime

KIWI FRUIT

kiwi fruit

KOHLRABI

kohlrabi

L l

LEEK

leek

LEMON

lemon

LIMA BEANS

Lima beans

LINGONBERRY

lingonberry

LOGANBERRY
loganberry

M m

MALABAR PLUM

Malabar plum

MALABAR SPINACH

Malabar spinach

MANDARIN ORANGE

mandarin orange

MANGO

mango

MANGOSTEEN

mangosteen

MAQUI BERRY

maqui berry

MORA DE CASTILLA

mora de castilla

MORINGA LEAF

moringa leaf

MULBERRY

mulberry

MUSTARD GREENS

mustard greens

N n

NAGAMI KUMQUAT

Nagami kumquat

NECTARINE

nectarine

NONDA PLUM

nonda plum

NORI SEAWEED

nori seaweed

O o

OKRA
okra

OLIVE
olive

ONION
onion

ORANGE
orange

P p

PAPAYA

papaya

PARSNIP

parsnip

PASSION FRUIT

passion fruit

PEA

pea

PEACH

peach

PEAR

pear

PERSIMMON

persimmon

PERUVIAN GROUNDCHERRY

Peruvian groundcherry

PINEAPPLE

pineapple

PLUM

plum

POMEGRANATE

pomegranate

POTATO

potato

PUMPKIN

pumpkin

PURSLANE

purslane

Q q

QUEEN ANNE CHERRY

Queen Anne cherry

QUINCE

quince

R r

 **RADICCHIO**

radicchio

 **RADISH**

radish

 **RAMBUTAN**

rambutan

 **RASPBERRY**

raspberry

RED GRAPES

red grapes

RED LETTUCE

red lettuce

RED PEAR

red pear

REDCURRANT

redcurrant

RHUBARB

rhubarb

ROMAINE LETTUCE

romaine lettuce

RUTABAGA

rutabaga

S s

SAPODILLA

sapodilla

SCALLION

scallion

SESAME SEED

sesame seed

SHALLOT

shallot

SNOW PEAS

snow peas

SOYBEAN

soybean

SPINACH

spinach

STAR APPLE

star apple

STRAWBERRY

strawberry

SUGAR APPLE

sugar apple

SUGAR BEET

sugar beet

SUGARCANE

sugarcane

SUMMER SQUASH
summer squash

SUNFLOWER SEED
sunflower seed

SWEET POTATO
sweet potato

SWISS CHARD
Swiss chard

T t

TABASCO PEPPER

tabasco pepper

TAMARIND

tamarind

TANGELO

tangelo

TANGERINE

tangerine

TARO

taro

TAYBERRY

tayberry

TOMATILLO

tomatillo

TOMATO

tomato

TURNIP

turnip

U u

UDUPI MATTU EGGPLANT

Udupi mattu eggplant

UGLI FRUIT

ugli fruit

UPLAND CRESS

upland cress

UVILLA

uvilla

V v

VALENCIA ORANGE

Valencia orange

W w

WATER CRESS

water cress

WATERMELON

watermelon

WHITE MULBERRY

white mulberry

WHITE RADISH

white radish

X x

XIMENIA

ximenia

Y y

YAM

yam

YARD LONG BEANS

yard long beans

YELLOW PASSION FRUIT

yellow passion fruit

YELLOW PLUM

yellow plum

YELLOW SQUASH
yellow squash

Z z

ZINFANDEL GRAPES

Zinfandel grapes

ZIZIPHUS JUJUBA

Ziziphus jujuba

ZUCCINI

zuccini

CEREAL

BARLEY
barley

FINGER MILLET
finger millet

MAIZE
maize

OATS
oats

PEARL MILLET

pearl millet

RICE

rice

RYE

rye

SORGHUM

sorghum

WHEAT
wheat

EDIBLE FUNGI

BAKER'S YEAST

baker's yeast

BUTTON MUSHROOM

button mushroom

CHANTERELLE

chanterelle

CREMINI MUSHROOM

cremini mushroom

ENOKI MUSHROOM

enoki mushroom

KING OYSTER MUSHROOM

king oyster mushroom

KING TRUMPET MUSHROOM

king trumpet mushroom

MOREL MUSHROOM

morel mushroom

OYSTER MUSHROOM

oyster mushroom

PORCINI MUSHROOM

porcini mushroom

PORTOBELLO MUSHROOM

portobello mushroom

SHIITAKE MUSHROOM

shiitake mushroom

TRUFFLE

truffle

WHITE BEECH MUSHROOM

white beech mushroom

HOT BEVERAGE

COCOA

cocoa

COFFEE

coffee

TEA

tea

NON- CEREAL GRAINS

AMARANTH

amaranth

BUCKWHEAT

buckwheat

CHIA

chia

QUINOA

quinoa

NUTS

ALMOND

almond

CASHEW NUT

cashew nut

HAZELNUT

hazelnut

MACADEMIA NUT

macademia nut

PEANUT

peanut

PECAN NUT

pecan nut

PISTACHIO

pistachio

WALNUT

walnut

PULSES

BEANS

beans

BLACK GRAM

black gram

CHICKPEA

chickpea

COWPEA

cowpea

DRY GREEN PEAS

dry green peas

GREEN GRAM

green gram

LENTIL

lentil

PIGEON PEA

pigeon pea

SPICES

ALLSPICE

allspice

BASIL

basil

BAYLEAF

bayleaf

BLACK PEPPER

black pepper

CARDAMOM

cardamom

CHILI PEPPER

chili pepper

CILANTRO

cilantro

CINNAMON

cinnamon

CLOVE

clove

CORIANDER

coriander

CUMIN

cumin

CURRY LEAF

curry leaf

DILL
dill

FENNEL
fennel

GARLIC
garlic

GINGER
ginger

MARJORAM

marjoram

MUSTARD

mustard

NUTMEG

nutmeg

OREGANO

oregano

PARSLEY

parsley

ROSEMARY

rosemary

SAFFRON

saffron

SAGE

sage

STAR ANISE

star anise

TARRAGON

tarragon

THYME

thyme

TURMERIC

turmeric

VANILLA

vanilla

www.ingramcontent.com/pod-product-compliance
Lightning Source LLC
Chambersburg PA
CBHW042006150426
43194CB00003B/142